WEST END ORGANIX

Ageless Beauty, Organic Health

Look and feel younger and healthier with our natural remedies products!

www.WestEndOrganix.com

Discount: 10% off of your order - Code *WEO2021*

PUMP IT UP MAGAZINE
LINKS

WEBSITE
www.pumpitupmagazine.com

FACEBOOK
www.facebook.com/pumpitupmagazine

TWITTER
www.twitter.com/pumpitupmag

SOUNDCLOUD
www.soundcloud.com/pumpitupmagazine

INSTAGRAM
pumpitupmagazine

PINTEREST
www.pinterest.com/pumpitupmagazine

PUMP IT UP MAGAZINE
30721 Russell Ranch Road
Suite 140
Westlake Village,
California 91362
United States

📞 (818)514 – 0038(Ext:102)
✉ info@pumpitupmagazine.com

Pump it up Magazine

TABLE OF CONTENTS

EDITORIAL
Page 5
6

DEBORAH LISS
Hollywod's Rising Star - Crafting Stories that Transcend Borders

REVIEW
How music for the roller rink impacted the clubs
10

WHAT'S HOT
L.A. Best Spots to visit

FASHION
How to start a fashion business
18

FITNESS
Get in shape!

TOPS TIPS
How To Create A Viral TikTok Video!

BEAUTY WELLNESS
What is micro-needling
Give Yourself A Mental Detox
27

MOVIES
Missing Barack

HUMANITARIAN AWARENESS
Women Lead Music Organizations You Need To Join

Pump it up
MAGAZINE

EDITORIAL

Dear Readers,

Our cover girl for the September 2023 issue is the talented Deborah Liss! In this edition, we delve into the world of Hollywood's rising star, Deborah Liss (photo credits Rory Lewis), and her remarkable journey in crafting stories that transcend borders.

We also explore how music for the roller rink has impacted the Cubs, share L.A.'s best spots to visit, and provide
insights on starting a fashion business, creating a viral TikTok video, and the benefits of micro-needling.

Don't miss our Missing Movies segment on Barack Obama's cinematic interests, and our tribute to women leading music organizations.

Thank you for being part of our community.

Enjoy the read!

Warm regards,

Anissa Sutton

CONTRIBUTORS

FOUNDER
Anissa Sutton

EDITOR
Michael B. Sutton

MARKETING
Grace Rose

PARTNERS

Editions L.A.
www.editions-la.com

The Sound Of L.A.
www.thesoundofla.com

Info Music
yourmusicconsultant.com

Deborah Liss

In the world of entertainment, the intersection of cultures often produces the most captivating stories. Deborah Liss, a talented actress, writer, and storyteller, embodies this dynamic fusion. Hailing from Brazil and carving her path in the glittering realm of Hollywood, Deborah brings to life a captivating tapestry of cultures that enrich her craft. In a recent exclusive interview, she opens up about her experiences, insights, and the delicate balance she maintains between acting and writing. Her unique perspective on blending genres and cultures provides a tantalizing glimpse into her exciting future ventures, promising to leave an indelible mark on both Hollywood and the literary world.

From Brazil to Hollywood: A Multicultural Journey

Deborah's journey from Brazil to Hollywood is a testament to the enriching power of cultural diversity. Growing up in Brazil, a melting pot of traditions and perspectives, she absorbed a rich tapestry of cultures. This early exposure sowed the seeds of appreciation for the intricacies of human experiences. Transitioning to Hollywood, another bastion of diversity, only deepened her storytelling prowess. Hollywood's increasing openness to foreign cultures, particularly Latin filmmaking, has made her journey all the more exhilarating.

Deborah draws inspiration from iconic figures like Carmen Miranda and Fernanda Montenegro, who have left an indelible mark on Hollywood while celebrating their Brazilian roots. Their talent has fueled her own artistic pursuits, driving her to create stories that transcend borders and reflect the vibrant diversity of our world.

"Catharsis": Where Writing and Acting Converge

In "Catharsis," Deborah seamlessly blends the roles of writer and actress, collaborating with her husband, director Ed Gallo, and cinematographer Ricardo Cohen. The film weaves the gripping tale of a workaholic woman's unexpected job loss, blurring the lines between reality and her deepest desires. Amidst a complex web of thoughts and emotions, an enigmatic hummingbird emerges as an unexpected guide, leading her on a transformative journey back to the vibrancy of life. This collaboration envelops the audience in the characters' journey, showcasing the powerful synergy when creative forces unite.

Deborah's multicultural background has profoundly influenced her acting and writing career. Growing up in Brazil exposed her to a rich tapestry of traditions, languages, and perspectives. This background has provided her with a unique lens through which she approaches storytelling. She weaves together various cultural threads to create narratives that resonate universally while celebrating the richness of our global heritage.

Exploring the World of Horror: "The Baby Seeker"

Horror is a genre known for evoking intense emotions, and Deborah is not one to shy away from its spine-chilling allure. "The Baby Seeker," a project born from her real experiences as a babysitter, offers fear and suspense in abundance. It's the kind of short film that leaves you wanting more, and there's already a plan in motion for a full-length horror feature.

Venturing into Literature: "The Diary of Madness"

Deborah's creative journey extends into the world of literature with her upcoming book, "The Diary of Madness." This thrilling narrative, to be published by WeCreate Publishing, revolves around a young woman and a doctor-scientist on a quest to cure a disease. What sets it apart is the unique reference the doctor employs—a diary containing the methods of one of the most inhuman minds of the 20th century. With intriguing characters and an exploration of the human psyche, this promises to be a compelling literary experience, delving deeper into character development, intricate plotlines, and the nuances of the written word.

Balancing Acting and Writing: A Harmonious Duality

As an artist, Deborah gracefully navigates the delicate balance between acting and writing. Rather than viewing them as separate entities, she sees them as interconnected. Acting provides insight into emotions, enriching her writing, while writing deepens her understanding of characters and storytelling, enhancing her performances. This harmonious duality allows her to pour her passion into both creative outlets, fueling more profound and versatile artistic expression.

Genre Exploration: From Drama to Horror

Deborah's work spans a variety of genres, but she finds herself most drawn to psychological drama and psychological horror. These genres allow her to delve into the complexities of the human mind, a theme that has always captivated her. Whether as an actress or writer, she immerses herself in research and understanding, aiming to create stories that peel back the psychological layers, giving the audience a deep and thought-provoking experience.

Collaboration and Unity in Filmmaking

Collaboration lies at the heart of Deborah's filmmaking journey. In "Catharsis," where she wore multiple hats, collaboration was essential. Working closely with her husband, director Ed Gallo, allowed them to align their creative visions seamlessly. The cinematographer Ricardo Cohen, producer Ana Silvani, and the entire cast added unique layers to the story, enriching the experience. From script to screen, their journey was marked by unity and a common goal to create something memorable.

Bridging Brazilian and American Cultures

Blending Brazilian and American cultures in her art is like painting with vibrant colors on a canvas for Deborah. This cultural fusion sparks her curiosity, leading her to explore fresh narratives and challenge conventions. It's about capturing universal emotions while celebrating diversity. Incorporating these influences into her work not only resonates with diverse audiences but also adds layers of authenticity.

Future Aspirations: Unveiling Untold Stories

Deborah's future brims with dream roles and projects that ignite her artistic passion. She envisions infusing Hollywood with the vibrancy of Brazilian culture and shedding light on untold historical tales from Brazil's past. Ultimately, she is drawn to narratives that blend her love for acting and writing with her dedication to amplifying Brazilian voices. Bringing the first Academy Award to Brazil for Best Picture would be a dream come true.

Messages and Themes in Her Work

Deborah's work is driven by a commitment to infuse every story, whether on screen or in her upcoming book, with a meaningful message or theme. She believes in the transformative power of storytelling to spark discussions, evoke emotions, and leave a lasting impact. Her aim is to craft narratives that resonate deeply with audiences, touching upon universal human experiences, inviting reflection, and fostering connections.

Advice for Aspiring Artists

Deborah offers valuable advice to aspiring actors and writers: cherish your uniqueness and hold onto your passion. Network, learn, and collaborate with those who inspire you, but avoid comparing your journey to others. Embrace setbacks as learning opportunities and persist through challenges. Let your passion be your guide, and remember that your authentic voice is your greatest asset. Keep refining your craft and enjoy the journey.

What's Next for Deborah Liss?

Exciting projects await Deborah on the horizon. "The Baby Seeker," a horror short film, is set to enter the film festival circuit. "Catharsis," their feature film, is nearing completion, and they eagerly anticipate sharing it through festivals. Deborah's book, "The Diary of Madness," is scheduled for release in August 2024, promising a compelling literary experience. Additionally, she is wrapping up another screenplay titled "Child Star," set to enter pre-production next year. With a whirlwind of creativity and passion, Deborah Liss is poised to share these projects with an eager audience.

In conclusion, Deborah Liss is a rising star in the world of entertainment, driven by her multicultural background, passion for storytelling, and a commitment to bridging cultures through her art. Her journey from Brazil to Hollywood is a testament to the power of diversity in shaping creative endeavors. As she continues to explore various genres and mediums, she leaves us with a promise of thought-provoking narratives that resonate deeply and enrich our lives. Deborah Liss is indeed an artist to watch, and her future endeavors are eagerly anticipated by fans around the world.

NEST ROOSTER VIDEOS

THE BABYSEEKER

NEST ROOSTER VIDEOS AND RCVIEW MEDIA AND WECREATE PRODUCTIONS PRESENT "THE BABYSEEKER" SCREENWRITER DEBORAH LISS DIRECTOR ED GALLO CINEMATOGRAPHER RICARDO COHEN PRODUCER ANA SILVANI PRODUCTION ASSISTANT NATHALIA COPPA ACTRESSES DEBORAH LISS AND TATYANA FIGUEIREDO CAMERA ASSISTANT ITALO BERTAGLIA MUSIC BY MARIACHAN AND KRAO SPECIAL VFX NEST ROOSTER EDITED BY NEST ROOSTER FILMED ON LOCATION AT LOS ANGELES CALIFORNIA

WWW.NESTROOSTERVIDEOS.COM

HOW MUSIC FOR THE ROLLER RINK IMPACTED THE CLUB

Moodymann's Soul Skate party embodies a long tradition where rollerskating and club music intertwine. We spoke with Kenny Dixon Jr., Traci Washington, Louie Vega, Danny Krivit and more on one of America's richest subcultures.

When you show up to Detroit's Northland Roller Rink during Soul Skate, you enter a different world. Thousands of skaters, along with a few hundred Moodymann fans, crowd onto the burnished hardwood floor. Look closely, and you'll observe nuanced regional skate styles honed in cities like Atlanta, Philadelphia and LA throughout the year. Skate scene DJs like DJ Arson play sub-110 BPM grooves to keep things rolling smooth. Detroit locals greet visitors like family. 80-year-olds put you to shame on skates.

Back in 2007, I showed up at Northland for the first Soul Skate. A free soul food buffet was on offer. Around 3 AM, the rink cleared out for "roll call," in which skaters showed off different regional styles—JB (James Brown-style skating) from Chicago, fast backwards from Philly/Jersey, Detroit's slide-heavy "open house" variant—while onlookers lined the rails. The event felt convivial, wholesome, about as far from the hedonistic Movement afterparty scene as you could get.

A decade and change later, Soul Skate is on the map as a national skate jam. 2018's edition was basically a small festival, with three rinks and a four-day programme that included things like an indoor picnic, a documentary screening and an adult prom.

"That was truly a mistake," said Kenny Dixon Jr., AKA Moodymann, on Soul Skate's escalation from local party to national festival. I spoke with him in the iconic, purple-curtained house he owns on Grand Boulevard, just across the street from Submerge, a noted local record store and headquarters for Underground Resistance. "Really it started out as, 'How can I put everybody in one room and focus on them buying my T-shirts?'" he said. "I wanna put everybody in there and smother them with my record label, my artists, my T-shirts. That was one of the ideas for Soul Skate, and then that flopped and people didn't give a fuck about my T-shirts or my product or my records. They were like, 'When's your next skate party?'" He laughed. "Yeah, it's its own monster now."

Since the mid-20th century, skating rinks have been an extraordinary staging ground for music and DJ culture, to say nothing of their importance within the civil rights movement and as a gathering space for black communities. As real estate in American cities becomes more scarce and rinks in black neighborhoods disappear, national skate jams like Soul Skate have become a crucial environment for a scene steeped in a tradition that continues to flourish.

Louie Vega, who fell in love with music and DJing as a teenage skater during New York City's early '80s skate boom, returned to the rink to DJ Soul Skate in 2014. "It's beautiful that Moodymann and the Soul Skate team stick to the roots and show where it comes from," he said over the phone. "Skating music has a lot to do with R&B and dance, just as much as discos and house clubs."

Style skating—a skate-dancing style that has splintered into hundreds of regional variants—got its start, in a roundabout way, in Detroit. Bill Butler started skating in 1945 at the Arcadia Ballroom on Woodward Avenue in Detroit on the one night black people were allowed in. At the time, skating rinks were typically scored by chintzy organ music, but on black nights they played records like Count Basie's "Night Train," "Ella Fitzgerald's "Do Nothin' Till You Hear From Me" and Duke Ellington's "C Jam Blues." Years later, as an air force sergeant stationed in Alaska, Butler won money for a pair of skates in a game of craps and started developing his signature "jamma" style, his movements mirroring the solos on the jazz records he'd skate to. He was assigned to an air force station in Brooklyn in 1957 and showed up at the nearest rink, Empire Rollerdrome, where mostly black skaters were rolling to live organ music. He approached the woman in charge and asked if she would play "Night Train." The needle dropped and style skating changed forever.

REVIEW

Legendary skate DJ and Soul Skate regular Big Bob Clayton refers to the now-closed Empire Rollerdrome as the "the birthplace of roller disco." Clayton, a New York native, has been DJing for 50 years.

"Most of the dance skating today, you see them holding hands and doing their moves, that's jam skating, that's Bill. That's Bill Butler all day," Clayton said. "I used to go to Empire in '69, but I wasn't worried about DJing in the skate world, I went there because I liked the hustle. I'd go there and dance, I'd skate for the first two hours, then the next two hours, I would hustle in the middle. We were all skaters and dancers, so a friend came to me once in '77 and say, 'Yo Bob, you ever think about DJing in the skate world?' I said, 'Nah man, I'm a club head, I like the club scene.'" He rattled off a list of legendary NYC haunts. "The Loft, Better Days, that's where I liked to be at... I've been playing club music and house music ever since the '70s. That's what I came from."

Clayton started DJing for skaters in '77, eventually landing enviable rink residencies at The Roxy, then at the mecca itself, Empire, both of which were outfitted with soundsystems designed by Richard Long, the legendary audio architect who built the systems at Paradise Garage and Studio 54 in New York and Warehouse in Chicago, to name just a few. Clayton began immersing himself in regional music and skate styles. The folk music anthologist Harry Smith used to have a party trick where he'd identify the county a singer was born in from one verse of a song. Clayton is the skate world equivalent.

"Every state and city had their own style," he said. Locking arms and traversing the rink in trains came from Detroit, for instance. "The hitch-kicking in the line came from Detroit. When you do a bow-legged move like this on your skates"—Clayton spreads his knees in his chair as though he's on skates—"it's called a grapevine. Came out of Detroit. If you want to see all the fast backwards stuff, that came out of South Jersey and Philly, and the Delaware area. I could talk to you about this for hours."

Beginning in the mid-'80s, Clayton traveled to rinks around the US. "I heard about wherever the adults were skating in each city and I would just go. They knew me from Florida to Buffalo, but a lot of cities didn't know who I was when I showed up. I would just pay my money, come in and stand around and I say, 'Oh, they play this here, or they skate like this to that music.' I took notes, I wrote stuff down. Bill gave me the incentive to do that. He traveled all over the country and brought this jamma technique. And that's how I got into the game. So for almost two decades, there was nobody out there but me, because nobody else knew what to do."

As Clayton made strides as a national skate DJ, he remained part of a coterie of NYC DJs and musicians that included Larry Levan, Nicky Siano and Boyd Jarvis. "Even though I was a skate DJ, they knew I loved club and house music, but I made my money in the skate world. Levan was the man. I'd leave Empire at four, five in the morning and go to the Garage. We learned from each other and I brought it to the skate world. When I first started taking out the bass and the highs, all the other DJs around the country at the rinks were like, 'What the hell does he keep doing to the music?'"

Clayton played the adult prom at last year's Soul Skate, holding court in front of a room of skaters who had switched out their wheels for heels and patent leather shoes. He attends every Soul Skate and regularly advises the team of 14 who run the event, which includes Rafael Bryant (Smooth Skatin Ralph), Demarco Bearden (Gadget), Joann Johnson (JoJo), Marcus Gavin (Fresh) and Maurice Dortch (Moe).

"Me and Kenny [Dixon Jr.], we met in the early '90s," Clayton said. "He was skating and hanging out then. This was before he had the record label... Kenny is a beautiful brother. He treats me like a god. He picked me up in a Suburban looking like I'm the president, being whisked through the city. They take good care of me and the respect is there."

The Soul Skate hospitality isn't only afforded to skate legends like Clayton. When I told Dixon Jr. I'd attended various Soul Skate events in 2018, he asked with genuine concern if I'd had a good time and apologized for how hot it had been. "It was way too many people last time," he said. "Apologies for that.

Speaking with Dixon Jr., who has agreed to only two interviews over the last decade, was never a sure thing. We were originally meant to meet up at Detroit Roller Wheels for a morning skate session he frequents, but he was due at DGTL Festival in Amsterdam the next day, and I was informed last-minute he wouldn't be able to make it. Undeterred, I drove out to the rink, a colourful building on an otherwise drab stretch of Schoolcraft St., on a cloudy Friday morning. Inside, a DJ played slow R&B jams like "Get To Know Ya" by Maxwell and "Insanity" by Gregory Porter. Regulars greeted each other with hugs on the side of the rink. A regal older couple glided by with one leg up in perfectly synced figure-skating style.

Traci Washington, Dixon Jr.'s right-hand, turned up a little before noon. After greeting a few skaters, we settled into a booth at the snack bar. I asked her how she got into skating.

"My daughter is now 21, but when she was in middle school, probably 13, they'd have skating trips," she said. "Often times during the day the rinks are reserved for school parties, so I went as a chaperone. I told Kenny about the party and he came over and once I saw what his body was doing on skates I was like, 'What in the world is going on here? What is that?' He was skating around children, jumping over kids that fell, simultaneously helping kids up, adeptly cutting through crowds of children. It just made me want to acquire that level—if not that level of skill—just to use my body as a form of art."

She went on: "No matter how tired he is he'll get off a flight from overseas and get to the rink that night. And he'll find skating sessions. If he's in London he'll find a place to skate. So it's a private way for him to enjoy himself. He is extremely humble, he doesn't promote himself or Mahogani Music." She gestured toward the rink. "These people in here don't know anything about Moodymann. They'll just say, 'Hey Kenny, how you doin'?' And he's always happy to see them and they're happy to see him."

At the rink, the swagger of Moodymann's persona slips away. It occurred to me that he's not interested in interviews because he's not interested in self-promotion. He's concerned with giving back to the community, whether it's throwing a BBQ in his backyard or handing out copies of his latest, unreleased LP. After I left Detroit Roller Wheels, I spoke to him on the phone. We talked about Soul Skate, Big Bob Clayton and that morning's skate session. He told me to come over to his house in an hour. Knocking on the door of his house on Grand, purple curtains blowing in the wind, felt like finally meeting a mythical, Wizard Of Oz-like character.

"That party is for Detroit," Dixon Jr. said. "We take an L every time, it takes us two years to recoup, save up and get money. But we're in the negative every year."

Due to the wave of rink closures, Dixon Jr. explained, skating has become a road trip culture. "For example, a lot of us skaters travel. But there are a lot of skaters that hear about the out-of-town parties and they can't travel. They don't have the means or the funds. We decided, why don't we just bring it to them? A lot of people ask me, how come you're not DJing or the regular rink DJ is not there? It's because, in a lot of ways, that's the same stuff we hear on a weekly basis. The idea of this here is bringing out-of-town people to Soul Skate is so, one, they can enjoy all the out-of-towners they don't usually get the opportunity to see, and two, so we can show them Detroit hospitality and make sure everyone's having a good time."

REVIEW

At each Soul Skate there's an unannounced headliner at Northland on Saturday night. In 2016, Dixon Jr., dressed immaculately in a white suit and straw campaign hat, introduced hip-hop legend Rakim. In 2018, a curtain dropped, revealing soul music legend Ronald Isley to a screaming, adoring audience gathered on the wood floor of the rink.

I asked Dixon Jr. if the Detroit skaters know he's a house music institution, jetting off to play festivals every weekend. "A few," he said. "It leaks out because you got the internet now. But have I officially come out and agreed to any of that shit? No," he laughed. "Going over there is providing a way for me to do things like this. To give people a concert they didn't even know was coming to them. They might have not seen Rakim. Or, you know, believe it or not, you got people that skate and will skip out on dinner or provide for their children, and I got a full course meal, you know? Try to keep it all night. I got food. Don't leave talkin' about you're hungry, I gotta go and I'm hungry. I got that for you. Don't leave cause you gotta go to a club to see some other thing. I got a concert for you. You ain't gotta go nowhere, it's all tonight baby. Plenty of motherfuckers from all around on the floor."

Back at Detroit Roller Wheels, Washington told me how the national skate community found out about Detroit and Soul Skate. "The largest party in the country was started by a woman from Detroit called Joi," she said. "It's this huge party called Sk8-A-Thon, held during labor day weekend in Atlanta. At these parties, sometimes they'd give the flyers back, they'd say, 'Detroit? No, we're not coming up there.' Because we're known to be aggressive. I mean, we have a very smooth style of skating, but you go to Royal Skateland, these people like to slide, they're very protective of their territory and if you can't skate that style, you might get injured. I would meet hundreds, I would dare say thousands of people who skate and eventually, they got interested in coming here and the word spread."

She continued: "We're one of the few parties that's truly diverse. That's because we're serving house, techno, Moodymann fans and the black skate community throughout the country. Some of the parties around America, they're so big, you can't rent skates, you have to have your own, because they don't want anyone to get injured. We make sure at Soul Skate you can rent skates, because a lot of the people who made this party possible are fans of Moodymann."

Soul Skate is unique in that Dixon Jr., known for producing and DJing club music, is now a recognizable figure within the black skate community. They recognize his afro and sunglasses from Soul Skate T-shirts, not the cover of Silentintroduction. But skating culture is about music as much as it's about style skating and community.

"A good skate DJ plays like your parents at home,'" Dixon Jr. said. "They play like back in the '70s when you went to a club and they played everything. See, I can go to a club, get down, sweat, 'Boy, that shit was exciting,' me and my friends we would get down. We would have a great time, talk to the ladies… At the skate rink, they gonna slow it down, they gonna break it down, they gonna break it all the way down. You ain't gonna hear no slow jams at the club no more. Back in the '70s and '80s they'd rock you for about two hours and they'll break it back down."

Dixon Jr.'s sprawling Prince collection was neatly displayed on the walls around us at his Grand Blvd. house. "You're telling me you're not gonna play no 'Do Me Baby' in this bitch? The fuck? Fuck that."

The style of DJing Dixon Jr. is referring to has its roots in New York City's post-disco scene, when the loose, slowed-down sound developing on singles from classic Big Apple labels like Prelude worked just as well, or better, at the rink as they did in the club. The development of skate music from the late '70s up to the present is intertwined with the roots of dance music, as nuanced and colourful as any sub-genre.

Bilingual Book Store
FRENCH - ENGLISH
www.bilingualbookstore.com

Are you a songwriter or composer struggling to protect your work and releases?
Well Bernie Capodici has done all the work for you in his new book
"Modern Recording Artist Handbook, How To Guide Simplified"

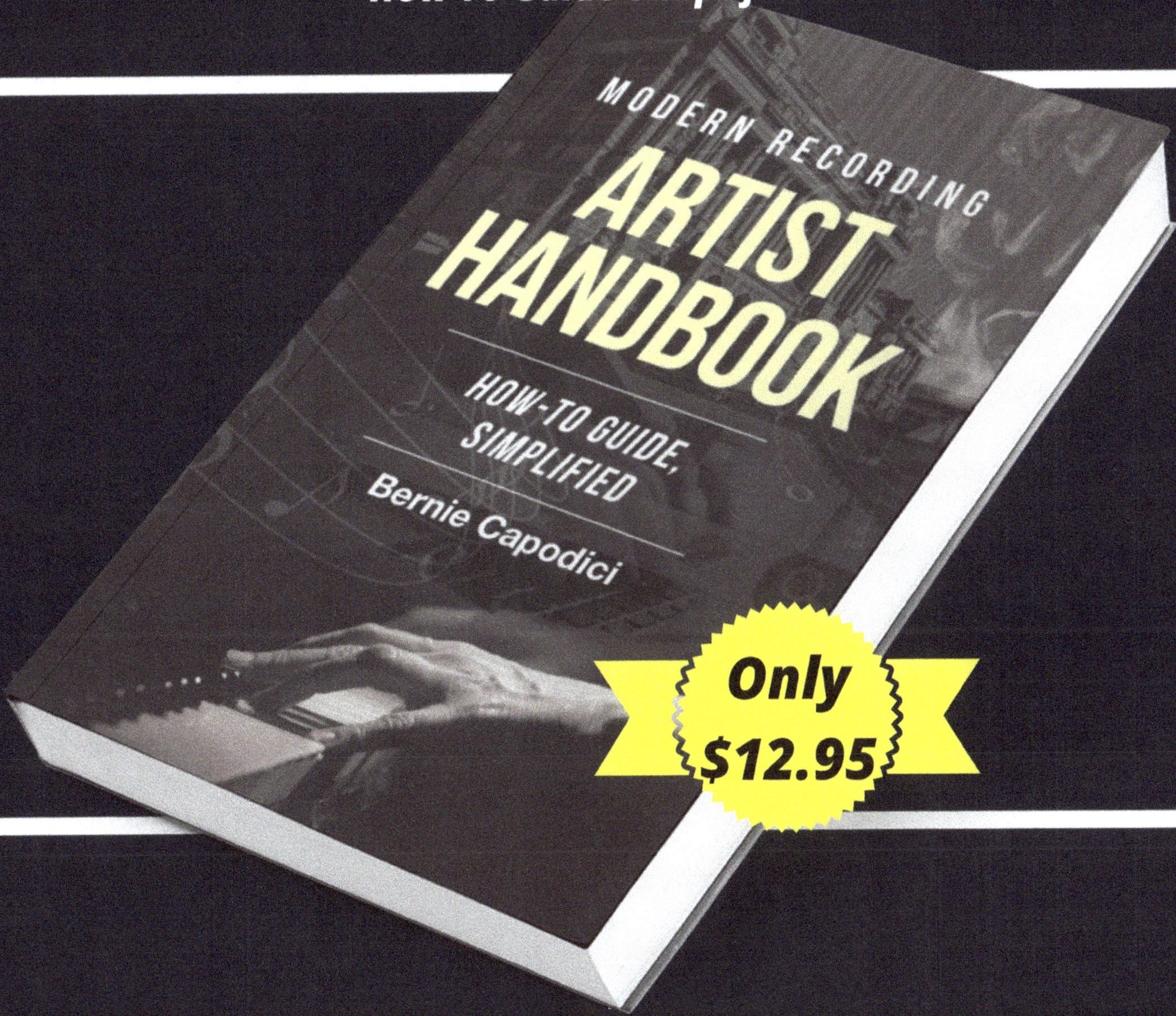

Only $12.95

MUST READ FOR INDEPENDENT ARTISTS

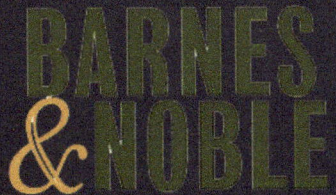

KINDLE $9.99 - HARDCOVER $22.95 - PAPERBACK $12.95

GET READY TO GO OUT! L.A. BEST SPOTS!

STROLL THROUGH THE STUNNING GARDENS AT THE HUNTINGTON LIBRARY

What is it? A historic library, museum and sprawling gardens that was the bequest of entrepreneur Henry E. Huntington.

Why go? The Huntington's distinctly themed gardens are easily the most stunning manicured outdoor spaces in SoCal. The library and museum are equally impressive, and reopen in mid-April; all require reservations.

Don't miss: Go for a stroll around the Chinese garden, which opened its massive expansion last fall. And make sure to see "Made in L.A.," which the Huntington is co-presenting with the Hammer Museum.

TRAVEL BACK IN TIME AT THE DRIVE-IN

What is it? About a half-dozen drive-in movie theaters in SoCal that are still going strong.

Why go? As theaters slowly reopen, it's one of the only ways to see a first-run movie right now that's not on your couch. But it's also tons of fun, cost effective and one of the few ways you can go out safely right now.

Don't miss: We particularly love the programming at Mission Tiki in Montclair. And look out for the occassional free screening or premieres thanks to familiar outlets like the ArcLight.

HAVE AN OCEANFRONT, ROADSIDE MEAL AT NEPTUNE'S NET

What is it? A postcard-worthy seafood shack on the Pacific Coast Highway toward the western edge of Malibu.

Why go? The fried ocean bites and weekend biker crew make Neptune's Net a unique destination. (Alternatively, dine up the coast with locals at Malibu Seafood, where the long line is worth the wait for fresh fish and seafood).

Don't miss: The famous spot is currently open with limited outdoor seating. So take your food across the street and park in the dirt patch by the water, with views of surfers and kite boarders.

L.A. UNLIMITED

APPAREL REPRESENTATION WITHOUT LIMITS...

- Corporate Brand Representation
- Brand Identity & Management
- Brand Consulting
- Trade Show Preparation & Participation
- Trunk Shows
- Private Label Sales
- Production Sourcing

L.A. Unlimited & Associates
30765 Pacific Coast Hwy STE 443Malibu, CA 90265

310.882.6432
sales@launlimitedinc.com

HOW TO START A HOME-BASED FASHION DESIGN BUSINESS

1. Think Like An Entrepreneur

To build a fashion business, you must be prepared to think and behave like an entrepreneur. You must come out of your design studio, meet those who know the business, and benefit from their experience. Find out how businesses work. Build solid relationships with a wide range of people such as manufacturers, investors, and buyers.

2. Know Who Your Clients Are

Without knowing your target customers or clients, you simply cannot move forward meaningfully when starting your fashion business. Remember that fashion industry and the market is vast, comprising of a wide section of the population from all ages and interests.

Who precisely are your customers amongst them? Do some research to know what trends of colors, styles, designs, etc do people like these days? What is the purchasing capacity of your customers? Answer such questions to get a dependable customer profile.

3. Start Small With One Product

One of the key points to consider is to start with just one fashion product. Many small business owners work on many product lines. But it is not a good strategy as it involves more time, money and management of staff and other things. Instead, start with one product line. Then, develop that product further so that people have faith in its design.

4. Set Right Prices

Another aspect of running a fashion design business successfully is setting the right prices. Find out the amount that your target customer is willing to pay. Then, calculate how much your business would spend on raw material and manufacturing.

5. Put Everything On A Website

People use the web to search and shop their choice of products or services. Your most of the potential customers make online search and then take a purchasing decision. A website for your fashion level is therefore crucial for its success. However, only a user-friendly site on the web works for businesses.

6. Have A Vision For Brand Identity

Your vision for the advancement of your company and its position in the market must be clear to you and your staff. This helps in building a brand identity that is different and unique from your competitors.

7. Promote Your Brand On Social Media

Social media is a powerful medium. A majority of your target audience of fashion business are on different social channels like Twitter, Facebook and Instagram. Without putting your brand on a wide range of social platforms, you cannot think of doing a successful business. Social media marketing is important to reach out to more and more consumers.

8. Distribute Flyers And Brochures

One of the effective ways to enhance your customer base of fashion design business is to distribute flyers and brochures. Flyers are generally short marketing materials consisting of one leaf of content.

Funk Therapy

| Funky | Trendy | Cool | Hip |

Wear The Music You Love!

Visit our merchandise store on our website:
WWW.FUNKTHERAPYMUSIC.COM
10% Discount code: STAYFUNKY

- Hoodies
- Crop Top
- Sweat Pants
- Bucket Hats
- Slides
- Mugs

UNISEX T-SHIRTS

Brown T-Shirt

GRAB IT NOW

Orange T-Shirt

GRAB IT NOW

Beige T-Shirts

GRAB IT NOW

Join our community
@funktherapy2

ANEESSA
MICHAEL B. SUTTON

I FOUND MYSELF IN YOU

OUT NOW

WWW.THESOUNDOFLA.COM

*Smooth Jazz Love Song
for An Essential Romantic Playlist
Capturing the joyful essence of
what it feels like
to love and be loved!*

FITNESS | 22 - 34

SLIM & SEXY

GET IN SHAPE!

TWO WEEKS PROGRAM

SLIM & SEXY

1 Legs, Stretching and warm-up, 25 Squats, 25 Sumo Squats, Repeat, March in place for 20 seconds Stretch muscles, Relax

2 Abs, Stretching and warm-up, 20 Standing Oblique Twists 30-second Floor Plank, Repeat above, March in place for 20 seconds, Stretch muscles, Relax

3 Arms, Stretching and warm-up, 25 Push-ups, 20 Wall Tricep Pushes, Repeat above, March in place for 20 seconds, Stretch muscles, Relax

4 Cardio, Stretching and warm-up, 50 Jumping Jacks, 30-second Sprint in place, Repeat above, March in place for 20 seconds, Stretch muscles, Relax

5 Combo, Stretching and warm-up, 10 Squats & 10 Sumo Squats, 10 Standing Oblique Twists, March in place for 20 seconds, 20 Push-ups, 25 Jumping Jacks, March in place for 20 seconds, Stretch muscles, Relax

6 Choose from Day 1-4 to work on your chosen area: Legs, Abs, Arms, or Cardio"

7 Rest!

Take a break! You deserve it.

TWO WEEKS PROGRAM

HOW TO CREATE VIRAL TIKTOK VIDEOS

KICK YOUR VIDEO OFF WITH A BANG

Set the tone and topic of the video within the first few seconds so that people understand what they're watching.

WHEN DECIDING ON VIDEO LENGTH, KEEP IT AS SHORT AS POSSIBLE

Unless you're telling a lengthy story that actually requires a full minute of video, keep your clips short and to the point. Tiktok looks at the average length of watch time compared to the length of the video as a method of evaluating quality.

USE TRENDING MUSIC OR SOUNDS

Whether you decide to do a voiceover or not, it's worth always including trending music in your videos. You can certainly choose your own songs, but TikTok is a social platform where people feed off the trends, so it's just substantially more likely that you'll do well if you use current trending songs. Always layer a song quietly in the background with a voiceover too.
Pro-Tip If you do want to use your own song, and TikTok won't allow it, you can just upload with your own audio, select a song, and set that second song to 0 volume.

TELL A STORY

Creating content that tells a story helps your audience relate to your product and see its relevance in their daily lives.

Editions L.A.

DIGITAL CREATIVE AGENCY

We Transform Your Vision Into Creative Results

Editions L.A. is a full-service agency based in Los Angeles. Our company is a collective of amazing people striving to build delightful services
We believe that is all about getting your message across clearly and with a "Wow!" thrown in for good measure.

Our Awesome Services

Branding

We build, style and tone your brand identity from the ground up.
We rebrand established bands, brands or businesses.

Merchandise Store
Website design and E-Commerce
Website updates

Digital Marketing

CD Cover | Banners | Logo design | Flyers | Brochures | Leaflets | Print ads | Magazine covers & artworks
Facebook / twitter / instagram / youtube artworks
| Book cover
Infographics | Icon Design |
| TshirtsProduct Labels | Presentation slides
Corporate graphics
Professional photo editing & enhancing
Redesign existing elements
YouTube Optimization and Monetization
Youtube Video Editing
Lyric Video and Advertising Design.

Publishing

BOOK COVER DESIGN
EBOOK FORMATTING SERVICES
and distribution on major platforms
(Amazon, Barnes & Nobles..)

Tell us about your dream and we will make it true!

Editions L.A.
7210 Jordan Avenue Suite B42, Canoga Park, California 91303, United States
info@edtions-la.com
Website: www.editions-la.com

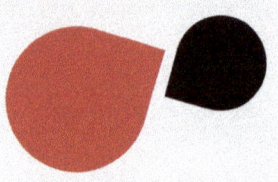

WHAT IS MICRONEEDLING FACIAL?
EVERYTHING YOU NEED TO KNOW

Microneedling. The minimally invasive treatment can be used all over the body—from scalp to ankles—to improve the appearance of scars, boost collagen, or encourage hair growth. Microneedling creates microscopic punctures in the skin.

MICRONEEDLING STIMULATES DORMANT HAIR FOLLICLES.

The stimulation of dormant hair follicles equals new hair growth, confirms Gohara. In a recent study, 100 test subjects were divided into two groups. One set was treated with minoxidil lotion, and the other received minoxidil lotion plus microneedling. After 12 weeks, 82 percent of the microneedling group reported a 50 percent improvement versus 4.5 percent of the minoxidil lotion-only group.

MICRONEEDLING CAN ALSO WORK TO REDUCE CELLULITE.

Alexiades works with a new crop of microneedling devices like the Profound by Candela. She uses the machine for crepe-like fine lines as well as sagging skin and cellulite.

YOUR DERMAROLLER PLAYS WELL WITH OTHER SKINCARE TREATMENTS.

Alexiades recommends pairing microneedling with topical treatments (like her 37 Extreme Actives anti-aging cream or serum) and lasers. "Often, we use this as an opportunity to apply anti-aging preparations that will penetrate better through the needle punctures. When you combine with topicals, you have a shot at some collagen building. When combined with radiofrequency, you can see tissue tightening over months," she says.

YOU NEED TO BE GENTLE ON YOUR SKIN AFTER MICRONEEDLING.

"Let the skin chill after microneedling," Gohara says. "For the rest of the day, don't wash the skin, expose it to high heat, sweat too much (that means no sun, no gym, no hot yoga)."

MICRONEEDLING ALONE ONLY GIVES TEMPORARY RESULTS.

Dr. Alexiades notes that a recent AAD study showed that microneeedling alone can only give temporary results that do not last. "As my over ten years of research has shown, you must combine microneedles with radiofrequency to get long term wrinkle and scar reductions and improvements in skin quality," explains Alexiades.

DOCUMENTARY

MUST WATCH
MISSING BARACK
A GENERATIONAL LEADER
COMING SOON

An intimate portrait of a young man destined to make history. Becoming Barack: Evolution of a Leader traces the early path of a man destined to make history and to be a catalyst for global change.

Features footage from three of the earliest known recorded interviews with Barack Obama: a 12-minute "lost" interview from 1993 by an aspiring inner-city documentary producer in Chicago which never aired; a 1990 clip from a news interview after he was elected president of the Harvard Law Review; and a 1986 WMAQ-Chicago news story about Obama's earliest success as a community activist, not aired since its original local broadcast 23 years ago. Also includes excerpts from Obama's audiobook reading of Dreams of My Father.

In the "lost" interview Obama was just 32-years-old, two years out of law school and championing the needs of some of Chicago's inner-city residents, a professor teaching constitutional law at the University of Chicago, a fervent community organizer and a newlywed who had not yet contemplated running for public office. Also features rare personal photos; interviews with family and a range of Chicago-area leaders in business and in grassroots community organizing who knew Obama intimately during his formative years, sharing personal memories and anecdotes; and historic photos and video footage of "Obama's Chicago in the mid-'80s through early '90s.

Becoming Barack reveals an unseen perspective of our new president at a time when he was finding his way, forming the ideals and principles that would guide him on a historic path. Even at this early time in his life, a vision of hope shines brightly and a desire to make this country a better place for all people

STUART A. GOLDMAN
EXECUTIVE PRODUCER

ROBERT YUHAS
PRODUCER/DIRECTOR

DOCUMENTARY

MISSING BARACK
A GENERATIONAL LEADER

CO-EXECUTIVE PRODUCERS: MICHAEL B. SUTTON, MITCH PERLISS, PAT BOONE

COMING SOON ON DVD
WWW.THESOUNFOFLA.COM/MISSINGBARACK

WELLNESS 30 - 34

MENTAL DETOX

- Drink More Water
- Take A Relaxing Batch
- Set Goals For The Next Month
- Learn A New Hobby
- Find A New Podcast To Listen To
- Write Out A Bucket List
- Get 8 Hours Of Sleep
- Read A Favorite Book
- Do 30 Minutes Of Yoga

@pumpitupmagazine

YOUR MUSIC CONSULTANT

"YOU BELIEVE, SO DO WE!"

We Can Help You To Grow Your Business

We are a monthly based service, we put faith in artists who has major potential, believed in them, and who are willing to spend their time and own money to work with us in building a successful music career!

Digital Marketing Services

SOCIAL MEDIA - STREAMING SERVICES - MUSIC DISTRIBUTION - PRESS RELEASE - PRESS DISTRIBUTION - PR

Radio Airplay and TV Commercial

TERRESTRIAL AND DIGITAL RADIO CAMPAIGN AL GENRES EXCEPT HEAVY METAL - CABLE TV AND MAJOR NETWORK COMMERCIAL

Licensing & Booking

CONCERTS, LIVE MUSIC, EVENTS, CLUB NIGHTS - RED CARPETS - FOREIGN LICENSING AND SUBOPUBLISHING

Why Choose Us ?

3 DECADES OF MUSIC BUSINESS EXPERIENCE
Platinum and Gold Records
MOTOWN RECORDS
UNIVERSAL
SONY
CAPITOL RECORDS

WE WORKED WITH:
Kanye West - Jay Z - Stevie Wonder - Michael Jackson - Germaine Jackson Smokey Robinson - Dionne Warwick - Cheryl Lynn - The Originals -

📞 **1-818-514-0038**
(Ext. 1)
Monday - Friday / 9am to 6pm

FIND US :

www.YourMusicConsultant.com
30721 Russell Ranch Road Suite 140 Westlake Village, USA
Email : info@yourmusicconsultant.com

WOMEN-LED MUSIC ORGANIZATIONS YOU NEED TO JOIN

these amazing organizations are taking action to expedite equality and empower women to step up, fight back and support each other to build a better future for all of us. It's incredibly scary entering an industry with such a large gender gap, but women in all aspects of the industry are building a landscape for the future where this is no longer supported. These badass, women-led organizations are doing the most to do their part in changing the future of the music industry.
Check 'em out. Get involved. Do your part.

WOMEN IN MUSIC

Women in Music is an organization with a mission to advance the awareness, equality, diversity, heritage, opportunities, and cultural aspects of women in the musical arts through education, support, empowerment, and recognition.

Their countless events celebrate the female contribution to the music industry and aims to strengthen the ties between the two for a better future for women in music. WIM believes all voices are welcome in the conversation about equality.

By joining WIM, you'll get access to in-person networking and educational workshops all over the world, online networking groups, directories, newsletters, forums and more to help you directly interact with the WIM community. Additionally, WIM provides resources to thousands of women in need in various stages of their careers.

Please visit:
https://www.womeninmusic.org/

SHESAID.SO

Established back in 2014, shesaid.so is a global network of women in the music industry. Made up of women from record labels, bookings, artist management, tech, creative and more, this organization curates and speaks on panels discussing the importance of the movement with hopes to inspire anyone who will listen.

Additionally, shesaid.so challenges the industry's outdated framework with their Alternative Power 100 Music List and works towards increasing the number of women who progress in their careers with their mentoring program, she.grows.

"shesaid.so started as and continues to be a space where members can openly ask for advice, share jobs and events, announce new projects and build community. There are currently over 3,000 international members in the global community and an additional 10,000 members across our 15 local chapters."

Please visit:
https://www.shesaid.so/donate

CHANGE THE CONVERSATION

Founded by three successful music executives, Leslie Fram, Tracy Gershon and Beverly Keel, Change the Conversation fights gender inequality in the music industry by providing support, education and a community of like-minded female artists and executives all working towards the same goal of equality.

Please visit:
http://www.changetheconversation.net/connect

HOW CAN WE EMPOWER WOMEN?

DONATE TO WOMEN'S SHELTERS

- Boost her self-esteem.
- Shut down negativity.
- Be open and honest.
- Advocate for female colleagues.
- Lead by example.
- Help provide clean water.
- Become a mentor.
- Support women-run businesses.
- Know your own worth.
- Fight against injustice
- Help a new mom adjust
- Show your appreciation for the women in your life.
- Keep a girl in school

SUPPORT ORGANIZATIONS THAT EMPOWER WOMEN